# From the Pew

**Conversations on Faith
from a Carpatho-Russian
Orthodox Lay Person's Perspective**

by

Serge G. Mihaly, Jr.

Carpathian Institute
Higganum, Connecticut
2018

© 2018 by Serge G. Mihaly, Jr.
All rights reserved. No part of this book may be reproduced in any form or by any electronic or mechanical means including information storage and retrieval systems without the express written permission of the publisher, except by a reviewer who may quote brief passages in a review.

Cover by Christopher Mihaly
Photo p. 73 © Rich Keen / DPRA, CC-BY-SA 2.0

Published by:
Carpathian Institute
184 Old County Road
Higganum, CT 06441-4446 USA

From the Pew:
Conversations on Faith from a Carpatho-Russian Orthodox Lay Person's Perspective
By Serge G. Mihaly, Jr.

Library of Congress Control Number: 2018961672

ISBN 978-1-938292-11-8

Publisher's Cataloging-in-Publication Data

Names: Mihaly, Serge G., author.
Title: From the pew : conversations on faith from a Carpatho-Russian Orthodox lay person's perspective / by Serge G. Mihaly, Jr.
Description: Higganum, Connecticut : Carpathian Institute, 2018.
Identifiers: ISBN 9781938292118
Subjects: LCSH: Mihaly, Serge G.--Religion. | Carpatho-Rusyn Americans--Religious life. | Christian life. | Orthodox Eastern Church--United States--History. | LCGFT: Essays.
Classification: LCC BX382 .M54 2018 | DDC 248.4/819--dc23

To my brothers Luke and Matt
who I've come to know and love even more these past few months.
I could not have asked for better.

'Now faith is the substance of things hoped for, the evidence of things not seen.'

Hebrews 11:1

# Contents

Foreword .................................................................. 9
Introduction ........................................................... 11
Renewal: The Wondrous Beauty of Confession
    and Communion ............................................ 15
Innocence and Tradition ....................................... 19
The Little Paths to Christ ..................................... 23
*'Nas'* (pronounced 'Naash') or 'Our People' ...... 29
In Their Footsteps ................................................. 33
Fishers of Men and Women ................................. 37
The Melody of Christ ........................................... 41
Perceiving the Unperceiveable ............................. 45
My Orthodox Faith and Politics .......................... 49
Orthodox Easter and Orthodox Christmas ........ 55
Sinful I Confess ..................................................... 61
The Best of Both Worlds ..................................... 65
A Christian's View of Hunting ............................ 71
The Awakener ....................................................... 77
The Story ............................................................... 81
Our Gifts ................................................................ 87
The Peace of Christ .............................................. 93
Acknowledgements .............................................. 97

# Foreword

As an Orthodox Christian priest of twenty-five years at St. John The Baptist Orthodox Church in Stratford, CT, I have endeavored to make the rich teachings and traditions of our Orthodox Christian faith accessible to the members of my flock, in a way that is personal and relatable.

I have found over the years that when I teach and preach using personal, real life experiences, I am able to more effectively illuminate the minds and heart of my parishioners.

I have also discovered that the learning process is greatly enhanced when the learner is actively engaged and encouraged to ask questions, and reflect upon how the teachings relate to their everyday experiences in life.

Several years ago, I added a new column in our monthly parish newsletter, titled *A View from the Pew*. It was my hope that I would inspire at least an occasional submission from my parishioners. Little did I know that this would be so well received.

One parishioner in particular, the author of this book which you now have in your hands, has kept me well supplied with thought-provoking and engaging vignettes related to his journey of faith towards the Kingdom of Heaven.

What our parishioners and I appreciate most about Serge Mihaly's writings is his down to earth, self-reflective writing style. When reading his essays, the reader is given a glimpse into the soul of the writer, and is also encouraged to reflect on their own experience. Coming from a peer, rather than the authority figure of a priest, the reader is challenged to think more deeply about their relationship with God in the context of their life both within and outside of the walls of the institutional Church.

I encourage you to find a comfortable chair in a quiet space and read as the Spirit moves you this beautiful collection of reflections from a man who is unabashedly, in the words of the poet Robert Frost, journeying down the road less travelled: a spiritual quest for the beauty and truth of the Kingdom of Heaven.

Fr. Peter Paproski
August 28, 2018

# Introduction

'From the Pew' is a collection of short stories I've written for my church paper. I've tried to capture the emotions and thoughts I carry with me and have carried with me for years as I attended this beautiful little church on Broadbridge Avenue in Stratford, Connecticut. Growing up in the 1960's, the church was the center of change within the diocese. Brought up as an altar boy and first grandson of the parish priest, Rev. Joseph Mihaly, I was instilled with a deep sense of pride for my faith, my ethnic heritage and my family. We were Carpatho-Russians, as my grandfather would call us, and we had a special tie to maintaining the faith of our ancestors. "Our People" fought hard to keep their faith when they migrated here, especially my grandfather. His battle was intense because he was so close to one of the original priests the Pope would excommunicate as he and others fought to keep our ancient traditions guaranteed us many years ago, Rev. Orestes P. Chornock who would later be named Bishop of the American Carpatho-Russian Orthodox Diocese of the USA. My grandfather accompanied Rev. Chornock to Constantinople when he was consecrated under the Greek Metropolitan, Athenagoras.

My grandfather also helped build the cathedral on

Mill Hill Avenue in Bridgeport, Connecticut. After the Catholic Church took the congregation's property and church on Arctic Street in Bridgeport, our people needed a new place to worship. Today, St. John the Baptist on Mill Hill Avenue stands as a proud testament to the hard work and faith of the Carpathian community. The church is no longer the home of the Bishop, but it has an active priest and dedicated attending members. Like many other churches, its numbers are dwindling, but its significance is not. Many of the same people who attend the Broadbridge church came from the Mill Hill Church coming to Broadbridge out of loyalty to my grandfather.

Whether it is at Mill Hill, St. John's on Broadbridge Avenue, the newer Cathedral in Johnstown, Pennsylvania or any of a dozen or more Carpathian churches across the nation, our people's stories are very similar, one of hard work and struggle and an undying dedication to Christ. If Orthodoxy is anything, it is consistent– as is the story of our people or *'Naš.'* We were mostly simple peasant farmers from the Carpathian Mountains in Europe who migrated to America to find a new, freer and more prosperous life. Some were sought by American factories, steel mills or coal mining companies, others were fresh off a ship filled with strange fellow travelers and still others were brought here by war or religious persecution. No matter how or why, they loved their new nation, sought to learn its language and become a citizen as fast as they could. To many, the transition wasn't easy, but it was worth the struggle as they carved out a little of the old world here in the form of the single most important part of their lives; their faith.

'From the Pew' is my remembrances and thoughts of our little church and her close-knit people. It is full of memories, thoughts and feelings, all of which I hope help shed some light on just how and why our 'little church' is so important to all of us. Christos Voskres!

July 12, 2018

# Renewal: The Wondrous Beauty of Confession and Communion

There are a number of experiences in life that can be considered transformational. Every day we learn something new that 'transforms' us changing our approach to life, some greater than others, but none, in my mind, are as powerful as the healing qualities of confession and communion. As Orthodox Christians we confess our sins to God and receive the Body and Blood of our Lord and Savior Jesus Christ in Communion. It is our most intimate union with God.

It has always been a mystery to me as to how God could actually 'suffer' death as God can't die. The answer lies in Christ, in His human ability to feel both joy and pain, for if God became human He could then suffer a human death and then, through his Divine nature, conquer death and rise again: a most profound concept, the very backbone of our Orthodox Christian faith. We are reborn, as Christ conquered the hopelessness of human death. Christ also brings us the hope of salvation and life eternal. Remarkable and beautiful.

The act of confession, though, is more than just a

recitation of words. It is a sincere examination of our lives, our consciences, our misdeeds and, most importantly, our separation from God. If we openly admit our sins we can begin to get 'back on track' in our lives with its very real struggles and very real achievements. Christ did not promise easy paths nor easy victories. No, but He did promise His love and salvation. And if we are to 'fight the good fight' that desperately needs to be fought we need Christ in our lives. We may carry our 'fight' to our jobs, our children's schools, our government and even within our families. Maybe our battle is to help a sickly child or a struggling elderly friend or maybe just pay our bills. All are worthy causes, for Christ is there beside us every step of the way. So long as we keep Him in our heart we will have the strength to keep fighting.

Finally, it is the joy experienced after confession and communion that is the most wondrous to me. It is also one of the most beautiful of all Christian experiences as the radiance of Christ's love becomes illuminating. There is a certain measurable relief in knowing that we can be cleansed of our sins no matter how serious. It is a rare opportunity to become renewed in Christ. Whether it is Pascha or any other day this renewal is like fresh water from a cool mountain stream to those who have become lost in the wilderness of our own sins. It lights our paths to new ways as old bad habits are broken. How wonderful it is to know that Jesus offers us this 'rebirth' if we only approach Him with sincere love and respectful fear as a disobedient child approaches a just and loving parent.

Let us then embrace the wondrous beauty of confession and communion knowing that it is a good thing, a very good thing. Something that opens our hearts, our eyes and something that renews our very souls.

October 5, 2009

# Innocence and Tradition

I do not have the training in theology like Father Peter Paproski or my brother Luke. Their knowledge and perspective on faith far exceeds mine. Like everyone else I see God through my own human eyes, trying earnestly to practice and follow Orthodox Christianity as taught to me by my parents, family and the wise words of our spiritual leaders. I struggle like everyone else and find Father Peter's description of Christianity as being a struggle very accurate. For me there is no state of perfection. That, I believe, is reserved for the next life, as God is the only being in the universe that is perfect.

I have, like many people, at one time or another questioned the existence of God. I have wondered in my darker moments if He was real as life at times seemed so desperate and lonely. It was only when the dark clouds left that I could reflect on what I had gone through.

Ups and downs, even deep downs, are not unusual in life; in fact they are a part of everyone's life. To think that we can escape bitterness, disbelief, tragedy, anger, resentment, and other forms of sin or disillusionment is simply an unreasonable expectation. In the end, it is how we cope with these that is important. Finding the right path through all the confusion is key. I can honestly say, for me, there is no greater coping mechanism than my belief in Christ. I have tried a few others in my life yet none have in any way been as reliable and effective as simple, honest faith in the Good Lord. Of course, faith is much more than just a coping mechanism. Properly practiced, it is a life.

I have also learned that Christ has never deserted me. He has stood by me, but never deserted me. And in those moment where He may have appeared absent in my life I have quickly come to realize it was not He that left me, but I that left Him. I can also say that to me, returning to a faithful life is an incredibly joyous experience. Nothing in my life has ever cleansed me like a confession so very needed. And nothing in my life has ever brought more peace to my mind and soul as returning to God.

Experiencing an Orthodox liturgy, to me, is one of the most beautiful and deepest of life's experiences. It not only refreshes my faith, it also reaffirms it. The combination of the music, the prayers, the icons, the incense and the spiritual traditions of the Orthodox service waken in me great peace and joy. But it is not just the service and prayers and songs that make it so special, nor is it the Epistle or the Gospel or even the Creed that stands out. For me, it is the sight of good men and women humbling themselves before God. It is a profound and beautiful thing, especially in a world that worships humanity over everything. This is the crux of our faith.

To worship God through Orthodoxy knowing the traditions and faith of our mothers and fathers and their profound love for Christ is also very important to me.

Orthodoxy is a faith of consistency, both theological and historical. It is also one of mystery. As a child it was their words and actions that gently showed me Christ's love for us. As a child I did not question what they said or did. Life seemed easy and faith natural. As an adult the world has grown so much more complicated. I am much more aware of the troubles and challenges in it. It is now more than ever that my faith, the faith that strengthened and guided my parents and their parents, strengthens and guides me. The same faith that got them through wars, poverty and plagues is also mine. If it was good enough for them, it is good enough for me.

January 28, 2014

# The Little Paths to Christ

Despite the rigorous challenges of life, Orthodox Christianity is a constant. Through weddings, births, and baptisms we call upon it to celebrate God's love for us, or bolster our human frailty through that same love. This is especially true in our little church on Broadbridge Avenue. We are a small church, but a church with strong faith, the kind of faith I believe the Good Lord approves of. We worship together as a family and comfort each other through life's challenges. We have a history that goes back several generations, back to men and women who came from a troubled continent to settle in the industrial city of Bridgeport, Connecticut, seeking personal and religious freedom and peace.

Full of extended families and 'old country' neighbors, many hard working and faithful people have worshipped here. Some worked in local factories manufacturing the planes that helped defeat the Japanese in World War II, while others contributed to the war effort working for General Electric in a building disguised as a large apartment complex. They came to America with their faith held closely to their heart saving their hard-earned nickels and dimes to build two beautiful cathedrals.

I remember some of these men and women as a young altar boy. I served before them and remember quite well that many had a hard time speaking English, but were distinctly proud of their new country. They were a quiet, humble people with a strong enduring Christian faith. On Friday nights during Lent I can almost hear their voices whispering their evening prayers. Often, when I am in church, I reminisce about them and my childhood here. There are larger, more ornate Orthodox churches, but none mean more to me than our own St. John the Baptist.

During a trip several years ago with my brother Luke, my niece and nephew and a few Orthodox friends, I had the great fortune to travel to Slovakia to visit an orphanage in a town called Medzilaborce. I will never forget the beauty of the rolling hills and the surrounding pristine forests, the legendary Carpathian Mountains with quiet little villages that, more than once, ran on both sides of a small trickling brook and, most of all, the sincere generosity of the people. In Slovak cities a hundredth the size of our own Bridgeport, we visited bishops and priests in beautifully decorated churches easily able to fit several hundred faithful in series of brand new pews. It was very satisfying to see our Orthodox faith firmly anchored there. I will also never forget the cherubic faces of those innocent little children we had come to visit, forgotten and cast aside by their parents, alone and cared for by the good will and grace of the Orthodox Church. We spent far too little time with them as they soaked up our wide smiles and small gifts we brought to make their days easier and more comfortable. Little ones barely able to walk, watched over by girls no more than 12 or 13, laughed and played with balls and toys that seemed so primitive by our wealthy American standards. Here everything was valued from simple friendships to simple foods. Most conversations had to be translated from Slovak to English and then back again, but usually it was the universal languages of love and kindness that mattered most.

We spent the last half of our trip with the children getting to know them, exchanging stories and warm, quiet smiles. The first half, though, was spent traveling. As each day passed, a friend of one of the local priests accompanied us. He served as our driver and guide as we traveled over busy highways and bumpy back, country roads. Here we found relatives in villages described in stories told to us as children by our fathers, mothers and friends. We watched little cars traveling to work and small trucks transporting food and other goods from Slovak factories and farms. Sometimes we drove for hours stopping to photograph the ruins of a hilltop castle or the site of a bubbling natural spring. We traveled through many small towns, one of which was the home of a distant cousin of my Aunt Kathy's: the World War II Marine hero Michael Strank, one of the men who helped place the American flag on Mount Suribachi on Iwo Jima.

On this trip, however, I will long remember one

special excursion. Tucked away amidst the mountain villages were tiny ancient churches, many built anywhere from the 16th to the 18th centuries. Often no more than the size of a small barn, there was one church that particularly stood out. It was a structure decorated with naturally weathered eight- to twelve-inch wide clapboards, darkly colored by centuries of harsh winters and bright sun. Hand hewn by Carpathian woodsmen, the architecture was simple, yet beautiful. The wood, cut from the surrounding forests, was also used to build the heavy church doors which were fitted with large steel locks most likely fashioned by a local blacksmith. Once inside, the village elder quickly began lighting candles. Soon the flickering light exposed dozens of beautifully dark and primitively painted round-faced Rusyn icons uniquely characteristic of the Carpathian culture. As I sat in one of the pews I noticed high above me and near the windows even more icons, all centuries old and priceless. In the front of the church was adorned an equally time-weathered wooden iconostas. My mind began to wander as I imagined Carpatho-Rusyn farmers and their families celebrating Easter with baskets of ham, horseradish, kielbasa, salt, butter and Pascha bread having been blessed by the local priest, singing the plain chant as we still do, watching their son or daughter marry or be baptized in holy water. What wonderful lives were lived here? What profound spiritual struggles were fought here under these beautiful icons?

As minutes passed we all found ourselves sitting silently

*Iconostasis of St. Michael's Church, Ladomirova, Slovakia*

inside this jewel of Carpatho-Rusyn Orthodox faith. As I sat there I could not help but compare this ancient little church to our own. There were, of course, the churches of the more populated cities, I thought. Newer, larger and much more ornate, most had towering icon screens and brilliantly glistening gold crosses, yet none could surpass the simple majesty of this one little church. It would be these little churches, scattered throughout the Carpathian Mountains, especially this one, that revealed the true nature of our ancestors' faith. They seemed to light a special path to Christ.

I am home now, but I would like to visit Slovakia again. I will always remember my time there and the sincere and faithful people who greeted us with open arms, most especially those precious little children. I will remember, too, the beautiful landscape, the hilltop ruins of castles and the sprawling Carpathian Mountains and its villages. Most of all, though, I will remember those beautiful village churches and the enduring faith of our ancestors. If I learned anything on this trip it was that our Orthodox faith has not changed and thankfully so. It was their faith that nurtured and steadied our ancestors and it is the same faith that nurtures and steadies us. Our Orthodox faith is indeed a constant, the one true constant in an often tumultuous and troubled world.

February 4, 2014

# 'Naš' (pronounced 'Naash') or 'Our People'

This past Sunday I drove to church traveling my usual route from Wallingford to Stratford passing by dozens of southbound eighteen-wheelers on their way to unknown destinations. The snow, which had piled up over the past few weeks, was finally beginning to melt, revealing objects not seen in weeks. As I entered church I instantly felt its usual blissful peace and reverence. I quickly dipped my hand in the tray of holy water, blessed myself and headed up to the choir loft where I took off my jacket and began adding what little I could to the ancient hymns everyone was singing.

It was a peaceful Sunday as most are. It is here in our church that our weeks begin and end. It is the Alpha and Omega in our lives, as we recharge our spiritual 'batteries' to start another week doing whatever it is we all do in our daily lives. This is certainly true for me.

After getting accustomed to my seat I looked around me and saw a choir loft filled with children all of whom were gently singing the plainchant choral hymns but a few feet away. I did not expect this, but remembered quickly that not a month before the same children had sung here as well. It was good to see them all standing at rapt attention and actively adding to the beautiful liturgy. There were no backup voices, just the little and not so little children led by an older choirboy, one of the priest's two sons. As I sat there and listened I thought it was a very practical way for our children to learn what it meant to live their Orthodox faith beyond prayers and attendance. It was one of our priest's thoughtful ways of bringing Orthodoxy to life and one I especially agreed with.

To me being a Christian is not just something we do blindly. It is, and is meant to be, an act of free will. It is a choice and one filled with personal challenges and sacrifice. As we are called to love God we are also called to serve him and many do in many ways. Some as priests, others as choir directors, others as altar boys, cantors, officers of the church, readers of the Epistles and the Creed, those who hold the troica, who build the Tomb at Easter or the Manger at Christmas and even those who sing and pray. As Christians every little act of faith is important as each act intensifies our love, individual and communal, and brings us closer to God. The same applies to the world outside our church, a task that is often one of the most challenging. I believe it is our 'service' within the church that strengthens us for our 'service' outside the church and is a lifelong effort. It is for this reason that I was struck by the events of this Sunday.

I had to ask myself today, though, what would our forefathers and mothers have said if they saw all here gathered together singing and praying according to the faith, the Orthodox Christian faith they brought here

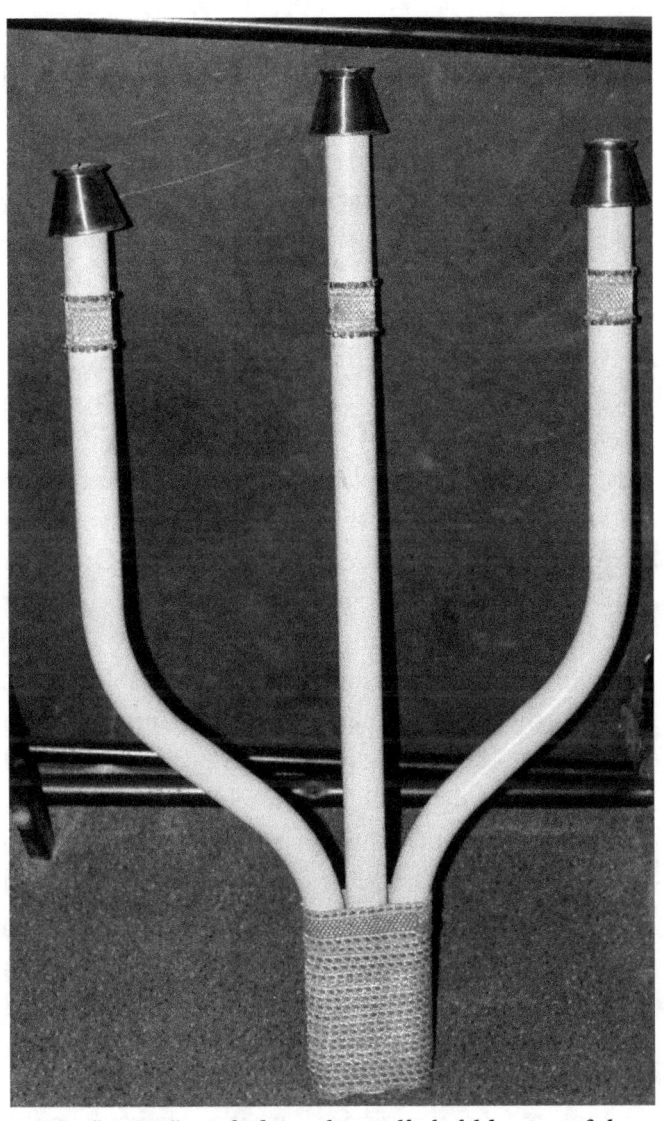

*The "troica" triple-branch candle held by one of the faithful during Liturgy.*

from the 'Old Country?' What were their deepest desires for us? It would be at the latter part of the service that I received my answer.

As our priest finished washing the chalice on the side altar and stepped back onto the amvon, he gently asked the newly elected church officers to stand before the iconostas. It was here they would take their oaths of office for the upcoming year.

As each arrived at the front of the church they quietly blessed themselves and spread out before the icons. It was then that I was struck by the thought of so many of our past parishioners and relatives. I looked down to see a very special group who, through their humble and quiet actions, actively and selflessly practiced their Orthodox faith. All of these men and women attended meetings handling portions of church life relatively few of us see, but without which the church would not be able to exist. They are the unsung heroes, the modern saints of St. John the Baptist. They do not have to sacrifice their time and effort, but they do. Much like our relatives before us they do the hard work that only can be truly appreciated from within. Although they do so without praise we should be proud of them as I am sure as our departed relatives and friends looking down upon us are. Their service, like the children's, is a fundamental part of our Orthodox worship, which keeps the church alive and fresh, new and reborn like Christ Himself. I believe this humble example of Christian service is what our forefathers and mothers wished for us to continue and are happy they have.

February 23, 2014

# In Their Footsteps

This year Friday night Lenten services brought back beautiful memories. As a child and teenager my mother and father took great care to bring me to church. It was difficult not to attend church for on those quiet nights my grandfather needed an altar boy. It was usually Billy and Sergei Bilcheck who would join my brothers and I as we dressed in our white cassocks and waited for the service to begin.

As we stood like soldiers at attention under the watchful eyes of Helen Rowland, a very unselfish and holy woman who supervised us behind the altar, we could see everyone who entered the church as they walked to the tetrapod, bless themselves, kiss the glass covered icon and find a seat in one the pews. As the church began to fill, other parishioners sat quietly and still others placed wrinkled dollar bills in wrought iron candle stands on top of which flickered their newly lit candle.

Soon one of us would help my grandfather prepare the *kadilo,* holding it just high enough so he could place a spoonful of incense on a burning charcoal lit but a few seconds before. My grandfather would then take the *kadilo* and walk through the church praying and incensing the icons and people. With each swing of his arms you could hear the gentle rattle of the *kadilo* chains

*Wrought-iron candle stands at St. John the Baptist.*

as the pungent incense wrapped itself around and above our heads in a cloud of sweet mist. With each swing of the *kadilo* the people would bow their heads and bless themselves.

Looking back now, I was mesmerized by the older men and women of the church, those who attended these Friday services with their short cut hair and colorful babushkas. Few knew English and those that did practiced it with a strong Slavic accent. Many of the men worked in local factories where they cut and shaped cold bars of rolled steel with lathes and milling machines. There was quiet strength to these people, strength I have always admired. It was this strength that brought them to our church tonight and to hundreds of Orthodox Greek Catholic churches around the nation on this quiet Friday night. But why were we here? Why did we attend?

My parents brought me up to be proud of our

heritage, both ethnically and spiritually. I have learned that there is a real and profound passion to being a Christian, a passion that goes beyond anything I have ever experienced at this or any other time of the year. Lent is the most moving and beautiful as I struggle to come to grips with my sinfulness and how far I have fallen short in this world. In the midst of my sinfulness just the thought of a good, just, loving and all-powerful God overwhelms me. How One so innocent and loving and perfect could have been betrayed and then crucified for our, my sins, always moves me to tears and enough so that I cannot sing. There is no more poignant time of the year for me than when, at the end of the service, we turn out the lights and sing. As a child I attended many such Friday night services week after week, enough to have my grandfather's voice beautifully still echo within me as he sang the '*Preterpivy*.' This is a good time of the year, too, as beautiful and cherished memories of deceased relatives and friends fill me with laughter and joy. How blessed I have been to have known them all.

Our faith is more than prayers and holidays. It is more than just sermons. It is a faith of all the senses, as Father Peter and other priests have said many times. It is much like what we are called to give to the Good Lord, our total and undivided love. It is on these Friday nights that I have realized more than ever the nature of our faith. It is humble, quiet and irrepressibly strong, a strength that can never be denied or defeated. I find it hard to express the feeling I have when I think of our ultimate relationship to God, His gentle and loving nature, His all-powerful essence. For me to sit and think of my relationship to Him as a mortal and imperfect creature I am overcome with emotion. I, like many, have seen the miracles of the tearing icon from Taylor, Pennsylvania, and have my own personal experiences from which to draw my belief from. For me He is very real and always will be.

The trains still rush past our church on those Friday nights, as do the same cars using Broadbridge Avenue as a short cut to some unknown destination. I am older now, much older and church and family and God mean much more to me. I do not know if those older members of our church with their short cut hair or babushkas felt or thought the same way as I did or do now. What I do know is it is their unconquerable faith and strength that has guided me as an Orthodox Christian moving me to preserve our Orthodox Christian faith. It is in the footsteps of those that came before that I try to follow, footsteps of those who joyously and steadfastly sacrificed so much that we too might know the Lord Jesus Christ through our Orthodox Christian faith.

April 12, 2014

# Fishers of Men and Women

According to the book of Matthew 4:18, the first Disciple, Matthew writes:

> And Jesus, walking by the Sea of Galilee, saw two brothers, Simon called Peter, and Andrew his brother, casting a net into the sea; for they were fishermen. He said to them, "Follow Me, and I will make you fishers of men." They immediately left their nets and followed Him.

It is a remarkable passage, as all passages are from the Bible, for there is so much wisdom and so much to learn in every word. This one, for me, has had particular significance especially in those moments of confusion, doubt or just everyday life. What do I mean? Well, as Christ called His apostles to follow Him, learn and then preach the Gospel, I believe we, too, are called. While the first twelve Apostles lived their lives in devotion to Jesus, we can too, and in a way that strengthens all of us.

While the fishermen in the Bible used nets to cast and gather their sustenance, we can as well, but with a tool we are much more familiar with. Today, most people I know use fishing poles to cast a line hoping to bring in a largemouth bass, trout or bluefish. It is a simple tool, but an effective one. But how does this apply here?

My grandparents, my mother and father and Christ Himself put great weight in prayer and, as we all know, prayer is powerful especially in the light of Christ's love and the Virgin Mary's intercession. In this I make a suggestion: Pick up your 'fishing pole' and cast, but this time cast a prayer.

Cast a prayer? Hmmm. Ok, let me explain. There are often times where I find myself struggling with my own troubles and crosses to bear, wondering how I am to overcome the challenges that I am facing. It is often in times like this that I see the 'innocents' and 'poor souls' that my grandfather and Christ Himself so often spoke of. The crippled old woman struggling to walk, the angry inner-city youth spilling hate, the persecuted Christians or others we see or hear about on television, a beautiful child in a wheelchair or the mentally ill that openly walk our streets, there are so many and all need God's Grace. These are the souls that we are called to 'cast a prayer' for and become the Lord's 'Fishers of men.' This is not just a nice thought or vapid act. It is deeply real and doing so changes us into true followers of Christ. For once we stop being people who see just our own troubles, we begin to see the world Christ sees, a world full of innocents, those who need saving, those who with tender hearts suffer far more than we do. They are lonely and the lost, those who do not have the advantages of life we too often take for granted. They hurt like us and need our help and desperately need the love of Christ and hence, ours too.

For what is God? It says in the Bible in 1 John 4:8: 'He who does not love does not know God, for God is love.' Love is indeed important.

The other day, after church I saw a man quite like one of the possessed souls in the New Testament Christ healed, cursing loudly with long uncut hair, talking to himself dressed in clothes that were too big and with what appeared to be his son walking painfully, but diligently behind. What problems they had I did not know, but I suddenly felt a great deal of empathy well over me. What could I do to help, I asked myself. I did not know. And then I thought, why not 'Cast a Prayer.' So, I did, asking God to help him, his son and his family. To enter in their lives and heal the evil which had so evidently taken hold. I left it to Christ, to our Savior with His great love and strength to heal this man and his family. It was a small thing, but not insignificant. I became an Apostle of sorts, what I would call a 'Fisher of Men.' But, how would this strengthen my faith? And then it hit me. Wouldn't it be wonderful if we noticed the downtrodden more, recognized who and how we might help those in need? We would no longer be blind to the sufferings of others obsessed with our own troubles, but, instead we would become one of the Lord's mighty soldiers doing Christ's work. I don't believe Christ wants us to prove our love for him by shouting from a mountaintop. Instead, what he does do is ask us to act out of sincerity and from an honest and loving heart.

The world is a formidable place, but where there is love

there is God, and where there is God there is always hope. How better to fight the 'Good Fight' than by fighting for those who need it the most, for those who Christ came to save, the downtrodden and suffering souls. For when we pray for others we also say a prayer for ourselves and learn that their needs are our needs, that their troubles are our troubles. It is in this shared humility and honesty that we truly practice our Orthodox Christian faith, finding we are never helpless, never real victims. Why? Because we are naturally victorious through Christ when we become Christ's 'Fishers of Men.'

December 13, 2014

# The Melody of Christ

I enjoy speaking with my priest. There is much to discuss as I make my way through this often confusing and troubling world. Father is always there to give me advice, not tell me what to do, but raise thoughts I may not have raised myself. We all have a unique and important relationship with him as he reaches out unselfishly in his grace-filled way.

One Sunday a few weeks ago Father came over to talk. He sat down and we began discussing a lesson he had presented to the youth a few minutes before. He mentioned the choir and how good they sounded that day and I agreed.

My place in the choir, like everyone else's, is a voice to be heard in union. I mentioned to Father that for me there is an important and unique place for everyone who sing even those who sing from the pews. While we contribute individually, the best music is found when we sing in rhythmic unison with each other. It is peculiar, though, because if you listen for one voice, you can pick it out amongst all the others and if you listen for an overall melody you can hear that, too. Both are gifts to God and are always sung with beauty and love.

I've noticed, too, that there is usually a leader, a cantor or someone who with confidence, passion and initiative guides the choir through the songs. When he rests his voice, it is up to the rest of the choir to 'take up the slack', to continue, to sing with our whole heart the beautiful notes of our liturgy. I admire my brother for being our cantor. He does this well. It is crucial that we sing at just the right tempo otherwise if we fall out of rhythm the music becomes tangled and chaotic. We are at our best when we sing together accenting each other's voices. There are times when the choir sounds triumphant especially on the holidays or right after Communion when my heart nearly leaps out of my chest. It is a wonderful experience and one that repeats itself every Sunday. Even when we pray for the dead there is such perfect poignancy that our singing of 'Eternal Memory' becomes much more a song of victory than anything else. For the times we fall short in our singing I don't believe God holds it against us. I believe He understands the limitations of our humanity and can see into our hearts. His desire is for us to do our best in sincerity and love and we do.

Father Peter recalled Saint Ignatius that day, an early second century Christian martyr and Bishop. While on his way to be sacrificed for his faith in Christ, St. Ignatius wrote several epistles. In one of them he very interestingly said:

> "Wherefore it is fitting that you should run together in accordance with the will of your bishop, which thing also you do. For your justly renowned presbytery, worthy of God, is fitted as exactly to

the bishop as the strings are to the harp. Therefore, in your concord and harmonious love, Jesus Christ is sung. And man by man, become a choir, that being harmonious in love, and taking up the song of God in unison, you may with one voice sing to the Father through Jesus Christ, so that He may both hear you, and perceive by your works that you are indeed the members of His Son. It is profitable, therefore, that you should live in an unblameable unity, that thus you may always enjoy communion with God."

Our liturgical songs are sung to God the Father through Jesus Christ. In a greater sense Christ leads us and we follow, but we do not do so mindlessly. One remarkable aspect of Christianity is that God respects us enough to ask us, of our own will, to voluntarily love and voluntarily follow Him. Christ's examples and teachings bring us to the possibility of a life we can emulate and work toward.

To return to the example of the choir, the same unified melody can also be viewed as our individual and joint living by Christ's rules. When the entire choir sings the sweetest it exemplifies our living and following Christ. When one of us fall out of tune it is a reflection of our fallen imperfection. Like the Lost Sheep, we return to the 'flock' when we return to the choir in harmonious melody. What beautiful 'music' we make when we all follow Christ. It is pleasing to us and to God.

It is very special to sing in church. It is something we can do alone in a pew, with the choir or silently to ourselves. Either way we are encouraged, but not forced to do so. During an Orthodox liturgy, music is a fundamental part of the service and is sung *a cappella*, or without instruments. I have my own favorite songs of which many are sung during the holidays especially at Christmas and Easter. There are, of course, other parts of Sunday services that I especially enjoy. Both holidays, though, are of great significance in the Church and are full of poignant emotions and memories, but let us not make these holidays the only moments of beautiful song. I believe God loves music at all times of the year and from each of us no matter what our ability. Let us sing together then, in unison and make God happy. While we may not always be in tune, I believe God knows we are trying and, more than that, he appreciates our efforts.

October 23, 2015

# Perceiving the Unperceivable

As Orthodox Christians we are taught to believe in the Holy Trinity, God the Father, God the Son and God the Holy Spirit. It is a fundamental part of that which makes us Orthodox Christians and whose full human understanding came about during the New Testament. While all three have existed since time immemorial, it is here that we were and are able to read and learn about all three. What I want to focus on, though, is the significance between the Father and the Son. Not the only significance of course, but one that I've thought about lately.

It is not uncommon for some to say they just can't comprehend God. He seems too fantastic, too impossible to believe in. Some say they can only believe in what they see. They cannot comprehend God, they say, unless He is Hollywood's nice old man sitting on a golden throne surrounded by beautiful white clouds. To them 'God' is an idea made up for the simple minded so they can rationalize things that they can't explain like gravity or the size of the Universe or the change in the seasons. It is their choice to believe whatever they choose. Christ doesn't want anyone to be forced to believe in Him. He respects and loves us enough to give us free will and does so for a reason. He wants us to decide for ourselves to believe in Him or not. On another level many of these same people say they cannot comprehend the idea of God or understand why He does the things He does. For me, the answer is we are not supposed to understand God for if we could, we would be God. Our concept of Him comes down to personal experience and faith. They are a part of the beauty and wondrous mystery of Orthodox Christianity.

What I was thinking lately, and what occurred to me significantly, is that God did not just send His Son to die for our sins conquering 'death by death,' he gave us something more. He gave us Someone we could 'touch, see and understand.' Like Thomas touching Christ's wounds that settled his doubt, Jesus Christ is the same to us. He is the 'real' thing, man, and is not some vague rationalization, guess or haphazard figment of anyone's imagination. He is both Man and God, a concept that startles reason, but still a real person we can identify with. Because Jesus was also man He looked like us and felt feelings like us, doing so while spending His first 33 years amongst mankind and mostly without recognition. Quite a remarkable feat for a being so different, yet not so different at all.

Until the other day, I really did not understand this. I took it for granted that Jesus is man and God and accepted the understanding that He came down from heaven to die for our sins, but not bridge the gap between God and man's perception of Him. This was a new thought, a different concept for me and one that opened my eyes

toward another significance and wonder of what Jesus is.

Others also explain God as the Creator of all, being seen in the unlimited complexity of life, the intricate nature of every inanimate object or living creature from countless grains of sand to one celled organisms to immense galaxies filled with billions of stars to long extinct dinosaurs and the evolutionary animal kingdom which followed. I have a hard time believing the world so intricate and organized came about 'accidentally' though a series of random mutations or through a 'Big Bang' theory. There is no 'Big Bang' theory in the Orthodox Church. To me the belief that the Universe was created by a large explosion is the result of mankind's oversized ego and a touch of insecurity that seeks an arrogant human centered explanation of the world.

Jesus Christ goes beyond this and brings Himself and God the Father home into our hearts, into our lives and more, into our human family. For me, this is enough.

February 22, 2016

# My Orthodox Faith and Politics

Politics and our Orthodox faith don't seem to have much in common. One focuses on an often-seamy environment full of struggles for power motivated by human centered arrogance. Just who to trust and not trust isn't easy to discern and is a lesson I am still mastering. Our faith, though, our belief in Jesus Christ and our salvation through His eternal victory over death is obviously very different. While Orthodoxy is embedded in the world, we are taught to follow Christ and take up our individual crosses. We are to love one another, believe in Him and be compassionate. While some see Christianity as a weakness, in an often ugly world of cruelty and selfishness our faith is a touchstone of sanity and goodness and a place of peace and regeneration for those who do believe. It is not easy when you are confronted with people or things that not just challenge you, but also work against you. Sometimes confrontation is unavoidable, but we do not have to fight alone.

For me, being an Orthodox Christian in politics has been a very serious challenge. Good people do exist, but so too are those who seek to benefit themselves, but act to gain fame, more power and, in many cases, fortune. How to be effective throughout all this, how to navigate through this is what I am looking to do. It seems a titanic challenge.

Currently I've associated myself with good people, people with the same values as I and people who care enough to fight and help. It gives me great comfort to know that they believe in what we are trying to do and some who have been doing this themselves.

I am a rookie in politics and I know it. What I have are my ideals, energy and what my parents and family and friends taught me. Most importantly, though, is what I've been taught by my faith and by Christ. Like Christ endured on the cross, we must also endure here as we fight for what we believe. It is not easy and I'm learning this well, but I know that others have succeeded and many with strong faith. My great-uncle Peter Zidovsky did as he served on the first Carpatho-Ukraine Legislature before Magyar forces in 1939 under orders from Hitler invaded the great Carpathian homeland. If he fought for what he believed in then I can as well. While I can look to my great-uncle, we can always also look to Christ who fought the greatest of all battles and overcame victoriously the greatest challenge of all: victory over death.

There were many times during the campaign while knocking on doors to talk to voters, or when I was looking for a treasurer or a manager or was ignored by a college buddy of mine who holds a high seat in government, that were the roughest. During these times it seemed there was nowhere to go and no one to go too. They were desperate days. During these times I prayed to

*Interior view of St. John the Baptist with stained glass window icon of Saints Constantine and Helena.*

God a very special prayer not in any prayer book I know of. A prayer I believe many of us say when all seems dark and dismal. For me it is always appropriate. During the darkest moments of confusion, I close my eyes and say 'Lord, help me do Your will.'

I do not pretend to know what God wants of me, for that is a unique journey for all of us. What I do, though, is to take away my worries and place them in a sincere request for help, not selfishly but as a servant of His will and love. What I've found is that God's will is often gentle and profound. At others times it is tough and steadfast. Only He knows what and how He wants me to be or do. Sure, I will make mistakes, but it is with greater confidence and faith that I approach the once seemingly insurmountable problem and often find, if not always find, a resolution that make great sense. It is not easy, but It is not meant to be. We still must live life and 'carry our crosses' but God helps us 'shift the burden on our shoulders' enough to take a few more steps. I have prayed this prayer many times.

I may have gotten the idea from a very famous man who, through his own experiences in politics and government faced his own challenges. He was also someone who referred to the Bible more than many historians want to admit. Abraham Lincoln was once asked how he withstood the pressures of the Civil War to which Lincoln replied, and I paraphrase, 'During the day I do my best to work to end the war and save the Union, but at night I say a prayer and ask God to take over while

I sleep.' It was this great faith that got this great man through some of our worst times in American history. It is in such light that I also ask God to lead me through the ethical, moral and legal challenges that confront me as I campaign.

One story before I go. I am relatively new to Wallingford, Connecticut, a nice town in which I am happy to live, but I am not a long-time resident. Trumbull, is, and always will be my hometown. Here in Wallingford few people know me and fewer have volunteered to help in my campaign to become a state legislator. Those who have are great people, unselfish and sincere. You would like them a lot. During the past few months I needed someone to help me with technology, but my request fell on deaf ears. I was at a dead end. Once again, I prayed to God my familiar prayer leaving it up to Him to help. One day, as I was walking down Main Street knocking on doors I came upon a young man, tall with glasses and carrying a computer satchel. I introduced myself and quickly got into a conversation about politics. By the time I got home I realized Kyle was exactly who and what I needed. Enthusiastic and bright, he has become a great asset to me and my campaign. God answered my prayer. Incidentally He has done so several other times too. I can only hope these are good signs, but again I leave it up to God to direct my path. What He has in store I do not know, but what I do know is that I look to Him for guidance and direction. I will falter at times, but so long as I do my sincere best as I've been taught by my faith, my parents, family and friends and look to Christ for guidance I am strengthened and recharged for whatever I will face. Endure. Yes, endure, but also look to Christ when we are confused no matter what the circumstances. I hope and pray I do well.

September 20, 2016

# Orthodox Easter and Orthodox Christmas

As I've grown older my perspective on life has evolved. More and more I recognize what my parents and grandparents spoke about when I was a youngster. I've also become more reflective realizing just how emotionally and spiritually 'cleansing' Church is. Sundays are beautiful in the Orthodox church, especially in our parish, but I am a bit biased. The aroma of the incense, the warm colored light that drapes itself across the tetrapod, the flickering candles, the sound of the

*The tetrapod decorated for Pentecost.*

choir singing age old hymns, the beautiful and unique iconostas and Father's voice reading the Gospel combine to create a spectacular experience that is penetratingly and comfortably real. This is even more profound during our major holidays of Christmas and Easter. There is an emotional significance though, between Orthodox Christmas and Orthodox Easter, a difference not in superiority, but in how we experience them. Let me explain.

With crusty snow piled on everyone's lawns, window shields and the sides of slippery roads, the warmth of Christmas and a winter fire appeared in my imagination as Father spoke about our faith tonight during one of his Wednesday night "boot camps." I thought of the manger scene and the baby Jesus wrapped in 'swaddling clothes' with Mary, Joseph, the Angels all watching and welcoming the newborn Messiah. I also thought of Christmas dinner, the smell of fir trees and our families. Christmas is indeed a time for family represented in the Holy family of the Christ child, the Virgin Mary and Joseph. Like Mary and Joseph who celebrated the newborn child's arrival 2000 years ago, we too, as Christian families, celebrate His arrival. The world was made wonderful that night and beautifully so.

While Christmas is a familial celebration of Christ's arrival, Easter is a little different. It is preceded by Lent, a 40-day period of fasting, reflection, of prayer and sacrifice, of almsgiving and the understanding of our sinfulness and the profound realization of the depth of

God's love. Why God would sacrifice His Only-Begotten Son for me, I don't know, but He did and He has. What great love, compassion and gentle strength He shows. I am often humbled to tears especially during our Friday night Parakalis services.

Like many of us, I was blessed to have parents so strong in their Orthodox faith that they cared enough about my brothers and me to take us to Friday Lenten services. The beautiful memories of my grandfather so poignantly singing *'Preterpivy'* still moves me. To this day, I can still see him kneeling before the altar singing with all his heart as if he were watching an exhausted and bleeding Christ carry His heavy wooden cross to Mount Golgotha where he would be brutally crucified.

Easter, unlike Christmas though, is not so much about family – although we still celebrate it with family and a Slavic feast of kielbasa, Pascha bread, horseradish, colored eggs, farmer's cheese, ham and other tasty delights. It is more, much more than Easter egg hunts and chocolate bunnies. Lent has ended and with it our personal trial in our own spiritual 'desert.' If we've sincerely strived to 'meet' Christ during Lent, we don't just recognize how blessed we are as a family of Orthodox Christians, we realize it as individuals. It is as individuals that we 'meet' Christ and it is as individuals that we experience the meaning of Easter and the most profound of all Christian tenets – the Resurrection of Our Lord and Savior Jesus Christ and His conquering of our physical and spiritual death by death. It is because of this that Easter is such a joyous time.

When those beautiful days arrive, and they will soon, let us wonder with grateful tears in our eyes and sincere love in our hearts at Christ's great love and mercy for us. Until then let us strive to move closer to God constantly realizing how blessed we truly are.

March 15, 2017

*Stained glass window icon at St. John the Baptist in memory of Father and Pani Mihaly.*

# Sinful I Confess

It seems as I get older, I am more and more aware of my sinfulness. Perhaps it is a function of my age and a growing recognition that I am no longer a child or even a young adult. My sons are all in or near their thirties and like many my age, I find myself asking 'where did the time go?' It seems it was only yesterday that my son Zach was learning to ride a bike. Now, he has two jobs, a wonderful fiancée and drives a truck.

For some, 57 isn't 'old', but it's not young either. Maybe, this newfound concern is a function of having more time to think, living by myself undistracted by a busy family life. Maybe it's the recent passing of both family and friends that has suddenly focused my mind on my own mortality and what that means. We are, after all, just as human and just as frail. Of course, our own passing is not something we want to think about. Like Benjamin Franklin once said, the only things that are guaranteed in life are death and taxes. In Connecticut, that goes double for taxes.

Having been stuck in the hospital and then a rehab facility healing from the effects of a replaced hip, I've had a lot of time to think. As a child and young adult, I saw and experienced life as an exciting adventure without any discernable rhythm except for the mostly happy wanderings of a blessed young man. My perception of God, of good and evil, of eternity, of my relationships with my friends, family, strangers and my future were not usually something I questioned. My view of life was dependent on the tenets of my upbringing. All seemed well, so why question it?

Today, as an adult, I've seen and learned more. Where I took life for granted before, I now realize how precious it is. I've been married, raised three good young men, have a beautiful extended family, graduated college, met great friends and experienced things I could never have previously imagined. I understand more now, both good and bad, and have a more realistic view of myself and life. Yet with all this new knowledge I actually understand less about a lot of things, which motivates me to ask questions. I now see behind the 'curtain.' I look deeper and find hidden and not so hidden meanings in things. This applies especially to my Orthodox Christian faith. As much as I believe, I too am human. I cannot take my salvation through Christ for granted and now find myself asking how I can strengthen my faith. The answer is to struggle, to keep struggling in the midst of life's distractions and there are many. There are answers, but there are no easy answers.

The devil may not appear to us as a red horned creature with a curved, pointy tail and long pitchfork, but he is here and only our faith in Christ and Christ Himself can defeat him. If there is anything I truly believe, this is certainly one of them. I see now why my parents did what they did, pouring themselves into their Orthodox faith more and more as they got older. Their experiences, too, taught them what I am only learning now.

November 19, 2017

# The Best of Both Worlds

Every year when December 25 rolls around, the country is enthralled by one of the most joyous holidays of the year. Christmas brings visions of 'sugar plums', Santa and last minute shopping sprees. To a large part of the Christian world it is a time to celebrate the coming of our Lord and savior Jesus Christ. Midnight masses are attended and songs are sung in honor and love to welcome the newborn baby. This is not exclusive to Western Christendom as many Eastern Orthodox churches celebrate at the same time, bringing together the two Churches. While there are many Eastern Orthodox Churches that celebrate Christmas on December 25th, our church goes by what is called the Julian calendar or 'old' calendar. With it our Christmas arrives later, January 7th.

Simultaneously, 'American Christmas', as my family refers to December 25th, sees countless stores suddenly become crowded, eye catching holiday ads, television shows of Santa and his elves and Frosty the Snowman and Charlie Brown cartoons. We become obsessed with buying toys, cars, sparkling engagement rings, new computers and more. Many will take a trip to New York City to brave the crowds and see the Rockefeller Center Christmas tree or the Christmas show at Radio City Music hall. The season is warm and busy, filled with good memories and holiday fun. All of this combines to create a wholesome sense of love and cheer. It is indeed a special time of the year.

I admit it, I love American Christmas and have many beautiful memories of family and fun. It is a fundamental part of my life, a time that has warmly marked my life. Yet, through all the joy, laughter and fun there is something missing. For me, the real reason for Christmas, Christ's birth, is often– too often– crowded out by gift giving, Santa Claus and a non-stop shopping frenzy.

As Orthodox Christians on Broadbridge Avenue we experience American Christmas. Santa visits our children and we become infused with the holiday spirit. We too enjoy snowy nights before warm fires, hanging decorations on our Christmas trees, family get-togethers, Bing Crosby's 'White Christmas' or Frank Capra's 'It's a Wonderful Life' and, of course, eggnog and mistletoe. December 25th is a beautiful holiday, but, for me, it has always been the first of a beautiful 'one-two punch', a precursor to a much more significant day yet to come.

Our Christmas, 'Russian Christmas', as my family calls it, comes several weeks later. It is on this day, January 7, where we joyfully celebrate and 'magnify' the birth of our Lord and King, Jesus Christ. We are not sidetracked with rushed shopping sprees or Christmas Eves devoted to wrapping presents or a visit by a gift-laden chubby elf and his eight tiny reindeer. No, we gather together in Church separate from the secular aspects of the season to sing and worship the 'reason for the season', the birth of Jesus Christ.

On 'Russian Christmas' we are singularly devoted to God, to the birth of Jesus, to the love of Mary and Joseph, to our traditions born through the sacrifices of our forefathers and mothers and their struggles to bring their Orthodox faith to America to grow and prosper. We sing beautiful liturgical songs with passion and love signaling the triumph of Christ's coming and all it foreshadows. We go to confession and communion, we hear the voices of our beautiful choir, the smell of incense as it rises high in the church, see a passionate Saint named Nicholas on the iconostas who as an early Bishop in our Church defended Christ's humanity and deism, and of course, greet each other with *'Christos Raždajetsja,'* answering with the refrain *'Slavite Yeho.'*

Our Christmas, held according to the Julian or 'old' calendar, is much more beautiful than 'American Christmas' because there is no confusion, no competing idea. Our Christmas is special because without dilution or distraction it is devoted to the birth of Christ. And while other churches celebrate it just as piously on December 25th, for me it's not the same. January 7th is solely focused on God's gift, His infant son and thus His promise of our salvation. This gift cannot be found in any television ad, nor is it located in a shopping mall or under a Christmas tree. This gift is from God's all-loving and generous heart.

I have always considered myself both blessed and lucky to be an Orthodox Christian. The people, the priests, the rich heritage and traditions and the beautiful familial love we share are all unique and so valuable. I have been blessed to celebrate both Christmases, one on December 25th and then on January 7th where we specifically celebrate God's great love for us in the birth of the baby Jesus. Both provide warm and beautiful feelings in me, different, but beautiful just the same. *Christos Raždajetsja!*

December 26, 2017

*Processional banner at St. John the Baptist.*

# A Christian's View of Hunting

It was during one of Father's house blessing visits that we started to talk, sharing the usual catching up of a parishioner with this family priest. We spoke about a lot of things, but one seemed to catch his ear and he asked me to write about it. So, I am.

I love nature, the woods, the smell of fall's fallen and moistened leaves, the colors of different trees, a wild rippling brook and the many creatures that live in it. I am always mesmerized by the delicate little birds that flutter and land on the many twigs and branches above the ground. Cardinals, juncos, starlings, robins, red-bellied and downy woodpeckers, brown headed cowbirds and an occasional grackle or two. The thought of how delicate each creature was, how they survived despite temperatures well below zero, has always intrigued me.

Chickadees are one-tenth the size of my fist, yet they jump here and there swinging their heads in little darting motions looking for any semblance of danger or food. I can barely stay outside a minute in the winter and these little birds stay out all day and night. Amazing. I marvel at how God protects them and has provided the necessary ingredients for survival and procreation. It reminds me of the Bible passage Matthew 6:26 that says 'Look at the birds of the air, for they neither sow nor reap nor gather into barns; yet your Heavenly Father feeds them. Are you not of more value than they?' The passage makes me realize that in the seemingly complicated world of nature, God's hand is always there guiding and providing what is needed despite our fears and insecurities.

My love of nature is more than just an ephemeral one, though. I love the ruggedness of it, the independence it demands and the freedom it offers. I also love the peace found there, a silent and soothing rhapsody of warmth and continuity, something rarely found in modern society. It is this same peace I find when I hunt. I've taken white-tailed deer, black bear, a caribou, rabbits and pheasants. I've hunted in Alaska, Canada, Connecticut, Virginia, New York and Pennsylvania, finding peace and relaxation in all. Bishop Orestes Chornock introduced my father to hunting and hence, my father to me and my brothers. With it came a deep and abiding love of nature, of man's evolving place within the natural world and the realization that we have a natural responsibility to care for it. One might argue, how could you kill something you love? This is a good question, and one I have wrestled with many times.

If anything, I believe an ethical hunter, especially a Christian, appreciates life as much if not more than the average non-hunter. While most people eat meat, fish or poultry, most Americans only see the end product of their food. They do not slaughter the animal and prepare it for market. The hunter knows the entire process and participates in it. He or she knows the cost of that hamburger, in this case a venison burger or steak – an animal's life. We study game every time we enter the woods, fascinated by the habits and ways of nature's wild creatures. In Genesis, after God made man it says 'He blessed them; and God said to them, "Be fruitful and multiply; fill the earth and subdue it and have dominion over the fish of the sea, over the birds of heaven, and over every living thing that moves on the earth." As gifts from

God we have a responsibility to handle them with care which draws right into my thinking on hunting.

Taking a life is a very serious and solemn act, something that hits at the very heart of a Christian. Life is precious, all life. It is because of this that as hunters, Christians know the practical aspects of taking game, that herds too large damage other species by over-browsing and eliminating certain plants that another creature would normally eat, stressing the entire ecosystem. In times of overpopulation with fewer available food sources, animals become weak, open to disease and in many cases death by starvation or predation. Die-offs can be dramatic, sometimes even threatening entire herds and, in rare cases, species. Ethical, science-directed hunting serves to reduce the size of various animal populations keeping them in line with the available browse. But, how does all this apply to a Christian?

If we understand that the creatures we harvest are gifts from God, which they are, then we must value them. Beyond this, too, we understand that it is our duty to dispatch them with the greatest of speed and least amount of pain. This is why we sight in our rifles and bows. To not do so is lazy and unethical and can cause unnecessary pain and suffering. There is no joy in the act of killing; maybe satisfaction in a good, fair hunt and accurate shot, but no joy. I've taken deer and know firsthand that the creature I brought home was created by God, that it served its purpose in life and I was blessed enough to enjoy its unique existence. Each creature has a role to play. While some are destined to live, feed and breed, others are destined to be food for another creature like a coyote, wolf, bear or, yes, man.

If we can consider the animals of the woods with such care and concern, how much more ought we apply to our fellow Christians and strangers we meet? We can go through life respecting each other and acting like Christ would want us to, or not. The choice is up to us.

March 15, 2018

# The Awakener

There is much to be proud of in our parish. Our God, each other, the deep history of our faith, the traditions, our parents, ancestors and youth. One aspect of Orthodoxy that a friend of mine recently said is that is quite remarkable how our faith has remained unchanged over the centuries. We not only have a history that is consistent in its beliefs; it's also true to Christ, hence the term 'Orthodox.' Filled with tradition and religious significance in each and every aspect of our faith, it has been the only real anchor in the Christian world despite numerous distractions and doctrinal changes by denominations.

Our parish, St. John the Baptist, now filled with many nationalities, was founded by a group of immigrants from the Carpathian Mountains of Eastern Europe. Referred to as Carpatho-Russia, Carpatho-Ukraine or Carpatho-Ruthenia, this area has been conquered and ruled by many nations including Hungary, Nazi Germany, Soviet Russia, the Ukraine and Poland. Because of the constant tumult, life for a Rusyn was not easy. Keeping our language, cultural traditions, religious practices such as a Slavonic liturgy and married clergy was a struggle depending on who and what was the latest opposing power trying to coerce the population

into national subservience. It took a great struggle by strong personalities to resist and pave a way forward for our ancestors. One of these personalities was a Greek Catholic priest by the name of Aleksander Dukhnovich.

Aleksander Vasilyevich Dukhnovich was a priest, poet, writer, pedagogue, and social activist. Born on April 24, 1803 and passing away on March 30, 1865, Dukhnovich would become known as the 'Awakener of the Rusyn people.' As much as William Shakespeare is identified as English, Ralph Waldo Emerson as American and Homer as Greek, Dukhnovich is Rusyn. Shakespeare gave us his sonnets, Romeo and Juliet, King Lear and other writings all of which are regularly studied by students; Dukhnovich's writings were not meant for entertainment nor have they been shared in most if any schools except maybe in Slovakia or other areas close to the Carpathians. Dukhnovich's poems were inspirational and spoke of the strength of his Rusyn nationality identity, culture, homeland, people, family and faith. His was a voice of rebellion and pride, a rebirth of an ancient Slavic people who'd been repressed by surrounding cultures.

Over the years Rusyn culture has been buried beneath Ukrainian, Polish and Hungarian influences which almost ended the Rusyn language and traditions. Dukhnovich would have none of this and while fighting for a separate Rusyn identity he was imprisoned under the Hungarian government. It was here, while in prison, Dukhnovich would write his most famous poem, one my father would often recite to his sons with his own brand of passion – *Ja Rusyn Byl, jesm y budu*' or 'I was, am and will remain a Rusyn.' It is this stubborn determination and national pride that burned in Dukhnovich's soul and much the same passion my grandfather Rev. Joseph Mihaly had for his heritage as he fought for our church and its people. *Ja Rusyn Byl'* would become the Rusyn

*Aleksander Dukhnovich*

national anthem. With writers, priests and other leaders adding to the cause, an independent Rusyn culture endured and was finally recognized.

It is from this history that our church was culturally born; that and the strength of our Orthodox Christian faith of which our people, the founders of this church, fought to build and establish here, starting in Bridgeport and then moving to other towns. For us it was on Broadbridge Avenue in Stratford.

In the early days of our parish, nationalities could be generally translated into different Christian denominations: the Irish to Protestantism or Catholicism, English– Episcopalian, Germans– Lutheran, Spanish and French– Catholic, etc. Today, our faith is much more religiously-centered in the sense that Orthodoxy is cross-cultural with the focus not so much on one culture, but on one's Orthodox faith. You don't have to be Rusyn to go to an Orthodox church that has roots in Carpatho-Russia or any other nation like Greece, Albania or Romania among others. Such a development has actually opened the doors wider to God, making us all true brothers and sisters in Christ. What once bonded and guided nations and villages of homogenous peoples, now bonds us as individuals and a Christian family no matter our cultural or historical differences.

And yes, I am a Rusyn– a Rusyn, an American and an Orthodox Christian and I'm proud of them all.

April 10, 2018

# The Story

When I was in ninth grade I remember taking a 3x5 piece of brass and cutting it into the shape of an Orthodox cross, complete with the short cross bar above the main beam and a slanted bar underneath. At the top, I drilled a small enough hole to fit a chain through and placed it around my neck. It was a combination of middle school shop class and pride in my Orthodox faith taught to me by my family that helped me create this one of a kind religious emblem. Not many kids had crosses that I remember back then, at least not triple bar crosses hung around their neck. About 2 ½ inches long and 1 ½ inches wide, it was difficult to miss as it hung from my teenage neck and was often the topic of discussion in school as fellow students would ask me what the bars meant. I took careful attention to tell 'the story.'

Most people who asked were very curious as to what those other bars were that made this cross so different than most others they'd seen before. For a moment my friends were focused on something other than rock music, sports or the latest gossip. It was a moment when time stopped as all eyes and ears were held still, waiting with bated attention to explain these curiosities.

There was the regular cross, I'd start, with the cross beam and long bar we all know. Above the main beam, though, was a shorter bar upon which was written 'King of the Jews', abbreviated in Latin 'INRI', a phrase written to mock Jesus as he lay bloodily nailed through his arms and feet high atop Mount Golgotha or 'the Place of the Skull.' For me the term 'INRI' is blazoned in my mind as it is inscribed on the large wooden cross behind the altar in our church on Broadbridge Avenue. As a child, I believe it was my grandfather who taught me the meaning and the rest of the story. 'Pa Pa', as I called him, Father Joseph to everyone else, had a way of gently explaining things which I would remember for the rest of my life.

That was just the first part though. The other bar, I continued, had two meanings. One, I said, was that there were two thieves on either side of Christ. One on the left and one on the right. The one on the right ridiculed Christ saying, according to Luke 23:39,

> "If you are the Christ, save Yourself and us." But the other, answering, rebuked him saying "Do you not even fear God, seeing you are under the same condemnation? And we indeed justly, for we receive due reward of our deeds, but this Man has done nothing wrong." Then he said to Jesus, "Lord remember me when You come into Your kingdom." And Jesus said to him, "Assuredly, I say to you, today you will be with Me in Paradise."

It was here I'd emphasize the message that if you believe in Him you will go to heaven and if you don't, you'll go to hell. Simple, but true.

The other meaning of the slanted bar came last, a testament to the unwavering faith of a believer who himself faced the barbarity of Rome's soldiers. St.

*Triple-bar cross on the grounds of St. John the Baptist.*

Andrew, the patron saint of the Slavs, was captured and sentenced to death by crucifixion. When faced with being crucified on a regular cross like Christ, he said he wasn't worthy and asked to have the bar slanted.

I don't think many expected the explanation to be in such detail, but it was and regularly left the questioner speechless. I don't think many people really know the story, at least this one, and the meaning of the triple bars that decorate and celebrate so much of the Orthodox Church and her faith. Triple bar crosses are seen in many places especially in church and many of our homes, and also on television especially when the news shows us pictures of Moscow's St. Basil's cathedral, but how many really know the significance of the triple bar crosses that augment the onion domes of that magnificent church or other churches for that matter? For many, they are busy symbols without specific meaning. I hope the story has changed that.

For me, I prefer a simple silver cross 2 inches by 1 ½ that hangs from my neck. Nothing fancy, just a quiet testament to the love and faith Christ had and has for all of us. Others like gold crosses, large or small, and there are many different styles to choose from, but whenever I tell the story I am transported back to my childhood as I stood and watched my grandfather serve during Lent. It was usually a Friday, the end of the week when as one of the altar boys I'd hand him a container of incense and with a silver spoon he'd drop a few crystalline grains on a slowly burning piece of charcoal as he sang our heartfelt

Slavic melodies and prayed so sincerely, while glancing up at the icons of saints and God above. As he got older, I could see increasing exhaustion in my grandfather's face, but I could also see his faith.

This was especially true on Good Friday as he read from the gospel describing Christ's march up Mount Golgotha to His crucifixion, death and soon to be resurrection. I could see Christ's blood drip down from His sweat-laden forehead as He struggled with the weight of His cross on His whipped and bleeding back. No story, no reading was more dramatic than the one my grandfather made that night, for it was the very core of our Christian belief: the struggle, the fight, the superhuman and enormous, but very human drive to complete His father's task. What a price to pay, what a burden to bear, what a sacrifice to make so we could enter His Kingdom.

I believe that the story of the Orthodox cross leads into this. It describes in detail what Christ suffered for us. It is an amazing story and one that purposely doesn't fit into today's secular world where everything we want is at our fingertips or waiting patiently at a drive through window. Most importantly, it puts into perspective so much we need to know.

June 6, 2018

# Our Gifts

My Aunt Marion, or 'Jo Jo' as we called her, had a favorite Christmas song. Each year she would love to hear "The Little Drummer Boy" play amid the soft fallen snow and twinkling lights of the beautiful Christmas holiday. With each note the song told a story of a loving little child whose gift to the Christ child was his ability to keep a beat on a drum he carried around his waist. While three kings travelled hundreds of miles to give the newly born Christ child Frankincense, Myrrh and Gold, this innocent little boy gave what he could, a gift of music and according to the song, upon hearing the drum beats the little Christ child smiled.

True or not, the message of 'The Little Drummer Boy' is very important. Each of us has some ability, some talent, no matter how mundane it may seem to us. To Christ, they are not. These gifts we can give to Christ in an act of love and respect. In our church we offer our gifts to Christ when we attend church, pray, sing or even bless ourselves. We help out with holiday breakfasts, picnics or tag sales. Some cook food, others serve trays of eggs and pancakes while others bring donuts, cheese, bagels, sweet deserts or egg salad for after-church brunches. Others help set up tables or clear tables, sweep the church, throw out the trash and even clean dishes. Others cook pastries

and *kapusta*, help out at soup kitchens, collect clothing or non-perishable goods at Christmas time, sell or buy raffle tickets, while others take the time to paint the sacristy or put in air conditioning for the relief and comfort of everyone. Whether it's a donation for an icon or candle or a quiet prayer in a pew, all and more are appreciated by God. It is not always *what* we do, but *that* we do, that counts, as each of us can offer something to the Lord no matter how small or insignificant it may seem to us. God sees.

In church, we light and hold candles, deliver the *kadilo* to Father, send our children to church school, read the Church Creed or serve on the church council. Father has his offerings too as he conducts services complete with beautiful ancient songs, prayers and the Eucharist.

We can also extend this to our daily lives. Whether at work or at home, as we strive to be the best Christians we can, although we all stumble, Christ still smiles at us. He sees everything we do or even try to do. God sees our hearts and takes note. As parents, our challenges are often very tough and even as children, young or older, the challenges these days are tough too. When we strive to help someone or even just focus our best efforts on the daily tasks in front of us we are giving of ourselves to our God.

Perhaps the greatest of gifts we can offer are our love and respect toward Christ and each other. Being mindful of our Christian responsibilities is also very important. Being kind to a stranger or a poor soul less fortunate than us, whether noticed or not, is yet another gift. What wonderful things can happen if we choose to make them happen and what wonderful gifts can we give Christ when we choose to?

The little drummer boy had no money to buy the Christ child a shiny toy or elaborate shawl. His offering did not have a monetary value like the three kings' gifts of frankincense, myrrh and gold. Its value came from his heart and in many ways was far more precious than all the diamonds and precious metals on earth. A spiritual gift is often much more important especially in a very secularly influenced world.

So, what is your 'gift' to Christ? What can you offer Him? What can you bring Him as He lays in that manger on that cool night surrounded by His mother and Father, cattle, sheep and the three Kings under a bright and twinkling star? Will you make Him smile? Maybe chuckle in delight? What talent do you have and if its not a talent then what else can you do out of love for Christ? Remember, the list is nearly endless as it is unique. It is up to you.

June 10, 2018

## The Peace of Christ

You can feel it in church, especially our little church in Stratford, Connecticut. It is the peace of Christ. In fact, you can feel it in any church if you sit quietly and alone. The truth is, though, that you are never alone in church. Christ and mother Mary are always there as are the many Saints and angels who grace the church, many of whom are pictured in the many ikons of the beautiful iconostasis, on the walls and ceilings in some churches.

For me though, I find a particular peace when I am in our little church in Stratford. Memories drift through the holy silence focusing my mind and heart. What greater peace is there than that of the peace of Christ? We may view the most spectacular of mountains, valleys or oceans, but it is not the same as a quiet church. I suppose anywhere you can hear silence you can find Christ, but the best and closest encounter is, for me, in our church. It is my direct connection with God and one which 'recharges my batteries.' If you listen closely you may 'hear' the voices past services, powerful chants and prayers all sung with a true humility before God.

If you've ever held vigil over Christ's tomb on Good Friday, you understand this well. Flickering candles, pungent remnants of incense, an occasional crack of blue and red glass, a shift in the old church foundation

and the sound of midnight cars passing the church all greet you as you sit patiently thinking, praying or studying the icons. There is a silent symphony of sorts as candles burn and flicker all around. Familiar sights of pews, service books, the triple bar cross, the amvon, fringed banners, our well-used red rug with its random spots of melted wax, carved iconostas, its stained-glass windows and troica, which sits in the back of the church, compliment the holy silence adding to the unique tone and atmosphere of our church.

On Good Friday interior lights are turned off, accentuating the many rows of red and blue candles, each lit in unison with a special prayer. Funny how the simple action of lighting a candle can bring out a person's piety. Many are lit before church and the rest after, but each is done with love and respect as a special petition to God. Whether we receive the results we wish for is not necessarily important. What is important is that in our confusion and concern we reach out to Christ, that we learn to accept Christ's will. As a wise man once said, '"No" is an answer too.' That is a part of the Christian understanding, that we do not control the world but must follow Christ for He and only He knows best.

Since my childhood Broadbridge Avenue has been my spiritual home. Before that, for much of my family it was the cathedral on Mill Hill Avenue in Bridgeport and before that Arctic Street. One is still active and the other now the home to another Christian faith. Both, though, have had their own unique atmosphere; their own remnant incense and memories of past services, ancient chants and prayers. I don't doubt their parishioners experience much the same as I have. One thing about Christ is that His love is peaceful especially recognized when we unworthily accept Communion, sing in the choir or pray the 'Our Father' and, of course, during those most quiet of times.

August 1, 2018

# Acknowledgements

I want to thank several people who have contributed to the publishing of this book. First, Father Peter Paproski for editing and posting the original stories in our Church bulletin. Father has been generously taking my contributions for years, often editing them for accuracy and grammar. He also submitted one article to the Church Messenger in Johnstown PA. Besides being a great parish priest, Father is also a good and valuable friend.

Thank you to my brother Father Luke Mihaly for his kind comments and suggestions. He is a great priest and brother. I suggest, if you can, listen to his sermons which are the most moving and heartfelt I've ever heard. I also want to extend a big thank you to my nephew Christopher Mihaly for the cover and back page. His talent in graphic arts has been a lifesaver for me and not just here.

Thank you to the parishioners of our church in Stratford for their kind comments. Your opinion is what counts so much to me.

Also, to my mother, father, aunts, uncles, grandfathers and grandmothers who raised me in the church and taught me to appreciate my faith and family. I have been blessed.

Finally, a big thank you to my cousin Michael Decerbo. Without his input and guidance, this collection of essays would not have happened. He helped me set up Word, my website blog and this book. Without his technical savvy I'd be lost. Thank you, Michael.

If I've missed anyone please forgive me. Publishing is the result of a team effort. Thank you.

Serge Mihaly  
July 20, 2018  
Woodbury, CT

www.ingramcontent.com/pod-product-compliance
Lightning Source LLC
LaVergne TN
LVHW051847080426
835512LV00018B/3120